# Mindful Money: Unraveling the Psychology of Wealth

Vana Hendy

# DEDICATION

With the help of Almighty God who lives forever,I dedicate this work to all who sees the need to do the right thing at the right time;YOU.

# CONTENTS

# ACKNOWLEDGMENTS

I would like to express my heartfelt gratitude to the individuals who have played a significant role in the realization of this book. Their support, guidance, and encouragement have been invaluable.

First and foremost, I extend my deepest thanks to Almighty God for his love and mercy,I also want to thank my family and friends for their expertise, inspiration, encouragement.Your wisdom, insights, motivation significantly enriched this project.

I am also grateful to My Lecturers for their editorial assistance, feedback, support during challenging times.Your keen eye and thoughtful suggestions have greatly enhanced the quality of this work.

A special thanks to my mentor for his technical assistance and research support. Your dedication and expertise were instrumental in bringing this book to fruition.

Finally, a heartfelt thank you to my readers. Your interest in my work is the ultimate reward, and I am truly grateful for the opportunity to share this story with you.

Thank you all for being a part of this journey.

Sincerely,


Vana Hendy.

# 1 THE DANCE OF DOLLARS AND DREAMS

In the vast landscape of our lives, few forces wicld as much influence as money. It is the silent orchestrator of our choices, the arbiter of our desires, and the silent companion in our journey through the twists and turns of existence. Welcome to the first chapter of "Mindful Money," where we embark on a journey to unravel the intricate web of the psychology of wealth.

## The Power of Perception

Money is not merely a tangible currency exchanged for goods and services; it is a potent force that shapes our thoughts, emotions, and behaviors. How we perceive money is deeply rooted in our upbringing, cultural background, and personal experiences. The lens through which we view wealth often determines our financial decisions, setting the stage for a complex interplay between the conscious and subconscious mind.

## Unraveling Money Scripts

As we delve into the psychology of money, we encounter the concept of "money scripts" – ingrained beliefs and attitudes about money that guide our financial behavior. These scripts are the silent scripts that run in the background of our minds, influencing everything from spending habits to investment choices. In this chapter, we will explore the origins of these scripts, questioning the narratives that may be holding us back from financial fulfillment.

## The Emotional Rollercoaster

Money is not merely a numerical value; it is laden with emotion. Fear, greed, joy, and anxiety are just a few of the emotional passengers that ride the rollercoaster of wealth. Understanding the emotional facets of financial decision-making is crucial for achieving a balanced and mindful approach to money management. We will explore the emotional triggers that often lead to impulsive financial decisions and strategies to navigate this intricate terrain.

### The Illusion of More

In a world driven by consumerism, the pursuit of "more" often becomes a never-ending quest. The psychology of money explores why we perpetually yearn for greater wealth and how this quest can lead to a cycle of dissatisfaction. Through case studies and real-life examples, we will unveil the illusions that surround the accumulation of wealth and challenge the notion that more money equates to more happiness.

### Beyond the Numbers

Money is not just about budgets, savings accounts, and investment portfolios; it is a reflection of our values, aspirations, and fears. In this chapter, we will encourage readers to look beyond the numerical aspects of their financial lives and delve into the deeper meaning that money holds for them. By understanding the psychological underpinnings of financial decisions, one can embark on a transformative journey toward financial well-being.

### The Influence of Childhood Narratives

Our earliest encounters with money often occur within the confines of our family dynamics. Childhood experiences, conversations, and observations shape the foundation of our financial attitudes. These narratives, sometimes inherited from generations past, can either empower or hinder our relationship with money.

## The Role of Society and Culture

Beyond the family unit, societal and cultural norms play a significant role in shaping our perceptions of wealth. Our understanding of success, status, and financial well-being is deeply intertwined with the broader tapestry of societal expectations. "Keeping up with the Joneses" is not just a colloquial phrase but a powerful force that can drive us to make financial decisions that may not align with our true values. This chapter delves into the societal constructs that influence our financial choices, encouraging readers to question and redefine their own definitions of prosperity.

## Money as a Reflection of Self-Worth

The psychology of money is not only about external influences; it is also an exploration of our internal landscapes. Many individuals tie their self-worth to their financial standing, creating a complex interplay between identity and net worth. By examining the emotional implications of money on self-esteem, we will unravel the layers that often obscure the true essence of one's worth beyond monetary measures.

## The Quest for Security

Security is a fundamental human need, and money is often perceived as a means to fulfill this need. The psychology of money delves into the intricate balance between the pursuit of financial security and the potential pitfalls of excessive risk aversion. Understanding the psychology behind our drive for security enables us to strike a balance between building a stable future and embracing the uncertainties that life may present.

## The Myth of Rational Decision-Making

Conventional economic theories often assume that individuals make rational financial decisions based on complete information. However, the reality is far more complex. The psychology of money delves into the quirks and biases that affect our decision-making processes. From the anchoring effect to loss aversion, understanding these psychological phenomena can empower readers to make more informed and intentional financial choices.

## The Connection Between Happiness and Wealth

A prevailing belief in modern society is that accumulating wealth is synonymous with achieving happiness. In this chapter, we will dissect this assumption and explore the intricate relationship between wealth and well-being. By examining the latest findings in positive psychology and financial well-being, readers will gain insights into how to cultivate a more harmonious and fulfilling life, beyond the pursuit of financial gain.

## Navigating Financial Transitions

Life is marked by transitions – career changes, marriage, parenthood, and retirement, to name a few. Each transition brings unique financial challenges and opportunities. The psychology of money provides a roadmap for navigating these transitions, helping readers anticipate and adapt to the changing financial landscapes that accompany different life stages. From setting financial goals to managing unexpected twists, this chapter offers practical guidance for embracing change with confidence.

## Mindfulness in Money Matters

At the heart of the psychology of money lies the concept of mindfulness. Being completely present and aware in the her e and now is a key component of mindfulness .Applied to finances, mindfulness can transform the way we approach budgeting, spending, and investing. This chapter introduces mindfulness techniques tailored to the world of money, providing readers with tools to develop a deeper understanding of their financial habits and cultivate a more conscious and intentional relationship with their resources.

## A Call to Self-Reflection

As we conclude this chapter, readers are encouraged to embark on a journey of self-reflection. Through introspection and thoughtful consideration, individuals can begin to untangle the threads of their financial narratives, identifying patterns and beliefs that may no longer serve them. This chapter sets the stage for the chapters to come, where we will delve into specific aspects of the psychology of money, providing practical insights and actionable steps towards a more mindful and fulfilling financial life.

As we embark on this exploration of the psychology of money, we invite readers to introspect, question, and challenge their preconceptions. "Mindful Money" is not just a guide to financial success; it is an invitation to a deeper understanding of the intricate dance between the mind and money. So, tighten your seatbelts as we unravel the complexities and unveil the mysteries of the psychology of wealth in the chapters that follow.

# 2 SETTING SAIL TOWARDS FINANCIAL WELLNESS

## The Art and Science of Goal Setting

Goals are the compass points that guide our financial journey. In this chapter, we will unravel the intricate process of goal setting, exploring the synergy between dreams and practical aspirations. Whether it's saving for a home, funding education, or building a retirement nest egg, understanding the psychology behind effective goal setting lays the foundation for a purposeful and fulfilling financial life.

## The Psychology of Delayed Gratification

Delayed gratification is the cornerstone of sound financial decision-making. This chapter delves into the psychological underpinnings of our ability to resist immediate temptations for the sake of long-term goals. Through real-life examples and behavioral studies, readers will gain insights into developing the mental discipline required to navigate the labyrinth of short-term desires and build a sustainable financial future.

## Overcoming the Fear of Financial Failure

Failure is an inevitable part of any journey, including the financial one. This chapter addresses the fear of financial failure, a paralyzing emotion that often prevents individuals from taking necessary risks or learning from mistakes. By reframing failures as valuable lessons, readers will be equipped to transform setbacks into stepping stones toward financial resilience and growth.

## Balancing Aspirations and Reality

Aspirations often outpace reality when it comes to financial goals. This chapter explores the delicate dance between ambitious dreams and practical constraints. By striking a balance between optimism and realism, readers will discover strategies to set achievable financial goals, ensuring that the pursuit of dreams aligns with the current resources and circumstances.

## The Role of Accountability

Accountability is a powerful motivator in achieving financial goals. This chapter introduces the concept of financial accountability, whether through partnerships, mentorship, or technology. By understanding how external factors can influence our financial behaviors, readers will learn how to leverage accountability to stay on course and achieve their desired financial outcomes.

## Celebrating Financial Milestones

Every journey is marked by milestones, and the path to financial wellness is no exception. This chapter explores the importance of acknowledging and celebrating small victories along the way. Recognizing achievements fosters a positive mindset and reinforces the connection between effort and success, motivating individuals to persevere in their pursuit of financial well-being.

## The Psychology of Adaptability

Financial landscapes are ever-changing, requiring adaptability and resilience. This chapter examines the psychological traits that contribute to financial adaptability. By cultivating a flexible mindset and embracing change, readers will be better equipped to navigate the uncertainties of economic shifts, personal transitions, and unexpected financial challenges.

## Cultivating a Vision of Financial Wellness

As we conclude this chapter, readers are encouraged to envision their personal definition of financial wellness. Through a blend of thoughtful goal setting, disciplined decision-making, and adaptive strategies, individuals can set sail on a journey towards a financially secure and fulfilling life. In the upcoming chapters, we will explore the intricacies of mindful spending, the psychology of financial habits, and the cultivation of a resilient mindset in the face of adversity. The voyage towards financial wellness continues, and with each chapter, we chart a course towards a more intentional and prosperous future.

# 3 MINDFUL MONEY: THE ART OF CONSCIOUS SPENDING

**Understanding Your Spending Mindset**
Spending is a fundamental aspect of daily life, yet the psychology behind it is often overlooked. In this chapter, we explore the intricate web of beliefs, values, and emotions that influence our spending habits. By understanding the deeper motivations behind our purchases, readers can cultivate a more intentional and mindful approach to spending.

**The Impact of Consumer Culture**
Modern society is saturated with messages encouraging consumption, fostering a culture of mindless spending. This chapter delves into the pervasive influence of consumer culture and its impact on our financial decisions. By developing awareness and critical thinking, readers can break free from the cycle of impulse buying and align their spending habits with their true values.

## The Psychology of Impulse Buying

Impulse buying is a common phenomenon, often driven by emotions rather than rational decision-making. This chapter explores the psychological triggers that lead to impulsive purchases and provides practical strategies to regain control. From creating spending plans to implementing waiting periods, readers will learn to navigate the allure of instant gratification and make more conscious spending choices.

## Cultivating a Mindful Budget

Budgeting is a powerful tool for financial control, but it requires a mindful approach to be truly effective. This chapter introduces the concept of mindful budgeting, emphasizing the importance of aligning spending with personal values and long-term goals. By incorporating mindfulness practices into budgeting, readers can foster a deeper connection to their financial decisions and make intentional choices that support their overall well-being.

## The Role of Gratitude in Spending

Gratitude is a transformative force that can reshape our relationship with money. This chapter explores how cultivating a sense of gratitude can influence spending habits. By appreciating what we have and focusing on experiences rather than possessions, readers can shift their mindset towards a more fulfilling and sustainable approach to consumption.

## Breaking Free from Emotional Spending

Emotional spending is often a coping mechanism for stress, boredom, or other emotional triggers. This chapter delves into the emotional aspects of spending, providing insights into recognizing and addressing underlying emotional needs. By developing alternative coping strategies and building emotional resilience, readers can break free from the cycle of emotional spending and make choices that align with their financial goals.

## The Art of Conscious Consumption

Conscious consumption involves making intentional choices that align with personal values and contribute to a sustainable future. This chapter explores the principles of conscious consumption, from supporting ethical businesses to minimizing environmental impact. By embracing a more mindful and intentional approach to consumption, readers can contribute to their own well-being while positively influencing the world around them.

## The Psychology of Financial Triggers

Every spending decision is influenced by a multitude of factors, including psychological triggers. This section delves deeper into the various triggers that prompt spending behaviors, such as social influences, marketing tactics, and the desire for status. Readers will gain insights into recognizing these triggers and developing strategies to navigate the psychological landscape of consumerism.

Financial Autopilot: Breaking Free from Habitual Spending

Habitual spending can lead to financial autopilot, where individuals make purchases without conscious thought. This part of the chapter examines the impact of habitual spending on financial well-being and provides practical steps to break free from these patterns. By cultivating mindfulness in daily spending choices, readers can regain control and redirect their financial resources toward meaningful goals.

## The Joy of Purposeful Spending

Purposeful spending is rooted in aligning financial choices with personal values and goals. This section explores the joy that comes from spending with purpose, whether it be investing in experiences, supporting meaningful causes, or contributing to personal growth. By embracing purposeful spending, individuals can derive greater satisfaction from their financial decisions and foster a sense of fulfillment.

## Strategies for Mindful Decision-Making

Making mindful spending decisions involves a conscious and deliberate approach. This part of the chapter introduces practical strategies for cultivating mindfulness in the decision-making process. From creating spending plans to setting spending priorities, readers will learn actionable steps to integrate mindfulness into their financial routines, leading to more intentional and satisfying outcomes.

## The Environmental Impact of Spending

Beyond personal considerations, spending habits also have a broader impact on the environment. This section explores the environmental consequences of consumer choices and encourages readers to consider the ecological footprint of their purchases. By making environmentally conscious decisions, individuals can contribute to a more sustainable and responsible approach to consumption.

## Navigating Peer Pressure and Social Spending

Social influences can exert a powerful effect on spending behaviors. This part of the chapter addresses the challenges of peer pressure and societal expectations, providing readers with tools to navigate social spending without compromising their financial well-being. By staying true to their values and setting boundaries, individuals can build resilience against external pressures and make choices that align with their financial goals.

## Embracing Minimalism: Less is More

The philosophy of minimalism advocates for simplifying life by decluttering both physical possessions and financial obligations. This section explores the principles of minimalism and its potential to reshape spending habits. By embracing a minimalist mindset, readers can find contentment in experiences over possessions and redirect their resources towards what truly matters.

## Crafting a Personalized Spending Plan

As we conclude this chapter, readers are encouraged to craft a personalized spending plan that reflects their values, goals, and intentions. This plan serves as a roadmap for conscious and intentional spending, empowering individuals to make choices that resonate with their vision for a purposeful financial life. In the subsequent chapters, we will delve into the psychology of saving, investing, and mastering the emotional aspects of financial decision-making. The journey towards mindful money continues, with each chapter offering new insights and strategies for a more intentional and prosperous financial future.

# 4 THE PSYCHOLOGY OF SAVING: NURTURING THE SEEDS OF FINANCIAL GROWTH

## Understanding the Psychology of Saving

Saving is the cornerstone of financial stability and growth. This chapter explores the psychological underpinnings of saving, from the satisfaction of building a financial safety net to the emotional resilience that comes with having resources for the future. By understanding the motivations and challenges associated with saving, readers can cultivate a positive saving mindset.

## Overcoming Procrastination and Building Consistency

Procrastination often hinders the establishment of a robust savings habit. This section delves into the psychology of procrastination, offering insights into the reasons behind delaying saving efforts. Readers will discover practical strategies to overcome procrastination and develop consistent saving behaviors, laying the groundwork for a more secure financial future.

## Setting Attainable Savings Goals

Effective saving begins with setting realistic and achievable goals. This part of the chapter guides readers through the process of defining and refining their savings goals. By aligning these goals with personal values and aspirations, individuals can stay motivated and focused on building the financial foundation they need to fulfill their dreams.

## The Role of Emergency Funds in Financial Well-being

Emergency funds serve as a financial safety net, providing a sense of security in times of unforeseen circumstances. This section explores the psychological peace of mind that comes with having an emergency fund and offers practical tips for establishing and maintaining this essential component of financial well-being.

## Saving for Short-Term and Long-Term Goals

Balancing short-term desires with long-term aspirations is a common challenge in saving. This part of the chapter delves into the psychological dynamics of managing immediate needs and future plans. Readers will gain insights into prioritizing savings for different time horizons, ensuring a harmonious and sustainable approach to achieving both short-term pleasures and long-term dreams.

## The Psychology of Automatic Saving

Automating the saving process can be a powerful strategy for building wealth. This section explores the psychological advantages of automatic saving, from reducing decision fatigue to harnessing the benefits of consistency. By incorporating automated saving into their financial routines, readers can effortlessly nurture their financial growth over time.

## Celebrating Savings Milestones

Just as with spending and budgeting, celebrating savings milestones is crucial for maintaining motivation. This part of the chapter examines the psychological impact of acknowledging progress and offers creative ways to celebrate various savings achievements. By recognizing and celebrating milestones, individuals can stay motivated and inspired on their financial journey.

## The Emotional Connection to Saving for Retirement

Saving for retirement carries unique emotional weight, as it involves preparing for a future that may feel distant. This section explores the psychological aspects of retirement savings, addressing fears and uncertainties while highlighting the emotional rewards of diligent retirement planning. By developing a positive emotional connection to retirement saving, readers can approach this critical aspect of financial planning with confidence and purpose.

### Coping with the Fear of Deprivation

Saving sometimes triggers a fear of deprivation, especially when it requires cutting back on immediate pleasures. This part of the chapter addresses the psychological aspects of overcoming the fear of deprivation. By reframing the narrative and focusing on the benefits of saving, readers can navigate the emotional challenges associated with making financial sacrifices for a more secure future.

## The Emotional Impact of Windfall Savings

Windfalls, whether unexpected bonuses or tax refunds, can have a significant emotional impact on saving behavior. This section explores the psychological dynamics of windfall savings, including the temptation to indulge in immediate gratification versus the potential for long-term financial growth. Readers will gain insights into harnessing the emotional energy of windfalls to bolster their overall savings strategy.

## The Role of Financial Education in Cultivating a Saving Mindset

Financial literacy plays a pivotal role in shaping saving habits. This chapter underscores the importance of financial education in fostering a saving mindset. Readers will discover the psychological benefits of understanding financial principles, empowering them to make informed decisions and build a strong financial foundation.

## Managing Financial Anxiety Through Saving

Anxiety about the future is a common emotional hurdle in financial planning. This section explores how saving can serve as a powerful antidote to financial anxiety. By focusing on concrete steps and achievable goals, readers can alleviate worries about the unknown and cultivate a more positive and optimistic outlook on their financial journey.

## The Connection Between Saving and Personal Values

Aligning saving goals with personal values enhances the emotional significance of financial planning. This part of the chapter encourages readers to reflect on their values and integrate them into their saving strategy. By establishing a strong connection between savings and personal values, individuals can find greater purpose and motivation in their financial pursuits.

## Navigating Cultural and Social Influences on Saving

Cultural and social factors significantly impact saving behaviors. This section delves into the psychological dimensions of cultural and social influences on saving, addressing how societal norms and expectations shape individual attitudes toward money. Readers will gain insights into navigating these influences and forging a saving path that aligns with their personal values and goals.

## Crafting a Savings Ritual

As we conclude this chapter, readers are encouraged to create a personal savings ritual. Whether it's setting aside a specific time each month for financial reflection or establishing a symbolic act tied to saving goals, a savings ritual can reinforce positive habits and provide a sense of ceremony to the saving process. In the upcoming chapters, we will explore the psychology of investing, risk management, and the emotional aspects of financial decision-making. The journey toward mindful money continues, with each chapter offering valuable insights and actionable strategies for building a resilient and prosperous financial future through the power of saving.

# 5 INVESTING MINDFULLY:NAVIGATING THE SEAS OF FINANCIAL GROWTH

## The Psychology of Investing

Investing is a powerful vehicle for financial growth, but it often involves navigating complex psychological terrain. This chapter explores the psychological aspects of investing, from the allure of potential gains to the fear of losses. By understanding these dynamics, readers can approach investing with mindfulness, making informed decisions that align with their financial goals.

## Overcoming the Fear of Risk

Risk is inherent in investing, and the fear of potential losses can be a significant barrier. This section delves into the psychology of risk aversion, providing insights into managing fear and making calculated investment decisions. Readers will discover strategies to navigate risk while maintaining a balanced and mindful approach to building a diversified investment portfolio.

## The Impact of Emotional Biases on Investment Decisions

Emotional biases, such as overconfidence, fear of missing out (FOMO), and loss aversion, can significantly influence investment decisions. This part of the chapter examines common emotional biases in investing and offers practical tools for mitigating their impact. By fostering emotional intelligence, readers can make more rational and disciplined investment choices.

## Setting and Adapting Investment Goals

Clear and realistic investment goals serve as a guiding force in navigating the investment landscape. This section guides readers through the process of setting and adapting investment goals, considering factors such as time horizon, risk tolerance, and financial aspirations. By aligning investments with personal goals, individuals can cultivate a sense of purpose and direction in their investment journey.

## The Psychology of Long-Term Investing

Patience and an eye on the wider picture are n ecessary for long-term investing. This part of the chapter explores the psychological aspects of long-term investment strategies, emphasizing the benefits of compounding returns and weathering short-term market fluctuations. Readers will gain insights into developing a resilient mindset that withstands the challenges of the investment journey.

## Building a Mindful Investment Portfolio

Diversification and asset allocation are crucial elements of a well-balanced investment portfolio. This section delves into the psychological principles behind building a mindful investment portfolio, considering factors such as risk tolerance, investment horizon, and financial goals. Readers will learn to create a portfolio that aligns with their unique circumstances and preferences.

## The Role of Patience in Investment Success

Patience is a virtue often tested in the world of investing. This part of the chapter explores the psychological impact of patience on investment success, highlighting the benefits of staying committed to long-term strategies. Readers will discover how patience can be a powerful ally in navigating market volatility and achieving sustainable financial growth.

## Leveraging Mindfulness in Investment Decision-Making

Mindfulness, the practice of being present and aware, can be a valuable tool in investment decision-making. This section introduces mindfulness techniques specifically tailored to the world of investing. By incorporating mindfulness into their approach, readers can enhance their ability to make clear-headed and rational investment decisions amidst market fluctuations and external pressures.

## Evaluating Investment Performance Mindfully

Regularly assessing investment performance is a crucial aspect of financial management. This chapter concludes by exploring the psychology of evaluating investment performance mindfully. Readers will gain insights into maintaining a balanced perspective, avoiding emotional reactions to short-term fluctuations, and making informed adjustments to their investment strategies over time.

In the upcoming chapters, we will further explore the emotional aspects of financial decision-making, including strategies for overcoming financial setbacks and cultivating resilience. The journey toward mindful money continues, with each chapter offering valuable insights and actionable strategies for building a resilient and prosperous financial future through the art of mindful investing.

# 6 RESILIENCE IN FINANCE: NAVIGATING SETBACKS WITH MINDFUL TENACITY

## The Emotional Landscape of Financial Setbacks

Financial setbacks are an inevitable part of life, and they can evoke a range of emotions from stress and frustration to anxiety and fear. In this chapter, we delve into the emotional landscape of financial setbacks, examining the psychological impact they can have on individuals. By understanding the emotions associated with setbacks, readers can cultivate resilience and develop strategies to navigate challenging financial situations.

## Embracing a Growth Mindset

A growth mindset is a powerful psychological framework that views challenges as opportunities for learning and growth. This section explores the concept of a growth mindset in the context of financial setbacks, encouraging readers to shift their perspective from a fixed mindset to one that embraces challenges as stepping stones to financial resilience. By adopting a growth mindset, individuals can approach setbacks with a positive and constructive attitude.

## Learning from Financial Mistakes

Mistakes are an inherent part of the human experience, and the financial realm is no exception. This part of the chapter delves into the psychology of learning from financial mistakes, emphasizing the importance of reflection and self-awareness. By acknowledging and understanding past errors, readers can extract valuable lessons that contribute to their financial growth and decision-making.

## Building Emotional Resilience

Emotional resilience is the ability to adapt and bounce back from adversity. This section explores the psychological components of emotional resilience in the face of financial setbacks. Readers will discover strategies to build emotional fortitude, including mindfulness practices, positive self-talk, and seeking support from a network of friends, family, or financial professionals.

## Reframing Challenges as Opportunities

Reframing challenges as opportunities is a transformative mindset that can empower individuals to turn setbacks into stepping stones. This part of the chapter explores the psychology of reframing in the context of financial setbacks, providing insights into how individuals can shift their perspective and uncover hidden opportunities for growth and improvement.

## Developing a Financial Recovery Plan

A structured plan is a crucial component of navigating financial setbacks. This section guides readers through the process of developing a financial recovery plan, considering both practical and psychological aspects. By breaking down the recovery process into manageable steps, individuals can regain control, build momentum, and work towards restoring financial stability.

## Seeking Professional Support

Financial setbacks can be complex, requiring expertise to navigate effectively. This part of the chapter encourages readers to seek professional support, whether from financial advisors, counselors, or other experts. By tapping into external resources, individuals can benefit from guidance, insights, and strategies to overcome setbacks and move towards financial well-being.

## Building a Mindful Relationship with Money

As we conclude this chapter, readers are encouraged to reflect on building a mindful relationship with money. By integrating the lessons learned from setbacks, embracing a growth mindset, and developing emotional resilience, individuals can foster a deeper and more intentional connection with their finances. In the following chapters, we will explore the psychology of charitable giving, legacy planning, and the holistic aspects of financial well-being. The journey toward mindful money continues, with each chapter offering valuable insights and actionable strategies for building a resilient and prosperous financial future.here.

# 7 BEYOND WEALTH: THE HOLISTIC DIMENSIONS OF FINANCIAL WELL_BEING

## The Multifaceted Nature of Financial Well-being

Financial well-being extends beyond monetary abundance; it encompasses a holistic perspective that integrates various aspects of life. In this chapter, we explore the multifaceted nature of financial well-being, recognizing that true prosperity involves more than just accumulating wealth. By understanding and embracing the interconnected dimensions of well-being, readers can embark on a journey toward a more fulfilling and balanced life.

## The Psychology of Charitable Giving

Charitable giving is a powerful force that not only benefits others but also contributes to one's sense of purpose and fulfillment. This section delves into the psychology of charitable giving, exploring the emotional rewards and psychological impact of supporting causes that align with personal values. By integrating philanthropy into financial plans, individuals can experience a deeper sense of meaning and connection.

### Legacy Planning: Beyond Finances

Legacy planning goes beyond passing on financial assets; it involves shaping and preserving one's values, stories, and contributions for future generations. This part of the chapter explores the psychological aspects of legacy planning, emphasizing the importance of leaving a lasting impact beyond material wealth. By reflecting on the legacy one wishes to leave behind, individuals can align their actions with their values and aspirations.

### The Intersection of Money and Health

Financial well-being and physical health are interconnected facets of a person's overall wellness. This section examines the intersection of money and health, considering the psychological impact of financial stress on well-being. Readers will gain insights into strategies for maintaining a healthy balance between financial and physical wellness, fostering a harmonious relationship between wealth and health.

## Cultivating Positive Relationships with Money

The quality of one's relationship with money can significantly impact overall well-being. This part of the chapter explores the psychological dimensions of cultivating positive relationships with money, emphasizing values, gratitude, and mindfulness. By fostering a healthy and conscious connection with money, individuals can enhance their overall sense of satisfaction and contentment.

## The Importance of Lifelong Learning

Lifelong learning is a cornerstone of personal growth and development. This section examines the psychological benefits of continuous education and skill development, highlighting how expanding one's knowledge can positively influence financial well-being. By embracing a mindset of curiosity and adaptability, individuals can navigate the ever-changing landscape of work and finance with confidence.

## The Role of Leisure and Recreation

Leisure and recreation are vital components of a balanced life. This part of the chapter explores the psychological aspects of incorporating leisure into one's lifestyle, recognizing the importance of rest and rejuvenation. By finding a healthy balance between work and leisure, individuals can enhance their overall well-being and derive more satisfaction from their financial pursuits.

## Connecting Financial Goals with Personal Values

Aligning financial goals with personal values is a key element of holistic financial well-being. This section guides readers through the process of identifying and prioritizing values, ensuring that financial decisions align with what matters most. By fostering a deep connection between values and goals, individuals can experience a greater sense of purpose and fulfillment in their financial journey.

## The Pursuit of Sustainable Happiness

Ultimately, financial well-being contributes to a more sustainable and enduring form of happiness. This chapter concludes by exploring the psychological dimensions of sustainable happiness, emphasizing the importance of balance, purpose, and meaningful connections in achieving a fulfilling and contented life. By integrating these principles into their financial plans, readers can embark on a journey toward lasting well-being.

In the upcoming chapters, we will delve into practical strategies for implementing these holistic principles into daily financial practices. The journey toward mindful money continues, with each chapter offering valuable insights and actionable strategies for building a resilient, prosperous, and well-rounded financial future.

# 8 SUSTAINABLE WEALTH: BALANCING PROSPERITY AND IMPACT

**The Dual Pursuit of Wealth and Impact**
Sustainable wealth is not just about financial prosperity; it encompasses the impact we have on the world around us. In this chapter, we explore the concept of balancing prosperity and impact, encouraging readers to consider the broader implications of their financial decisions. By aligning wealth creation with positive contributions to society and the environment, individuals can cultivate a more sustainable and meaningful form of prosperity.

**Understanding the Ripple Effect of Financial Choices**
Financial choices have a ripple effect, influencing not only individual well-being but also the communities and ecosystems we inhabit. This section delves into the

interconnected nature of financial decisions, examining how choices in spending, investing, and philanthropy can create a positive ripple effect. By understanding the broader implications of their actions, readers can make choices that contribute to both personal and societal well-being.

## The Power of Ethical and Sustainable Investing

Investing with ethics and sustainability in mind is a powerful way to align financial goals with positive impact. This part of the chapter explores the principles of ethical and sustainable investing, considering factors such as environmental, social, and governance (ESG) criteria. Readers will gain insights into how investment choices can be a force for positive change while still achieving financial returns.

## Incorporating Social Responsibility into Financial Plans

Social responsibility goes beyond philanthropy; it involves integrating values and impact considerations into financial plans. This section provides practical guidance on how individuals can incorporate social responsibility into their financial strategies. By aligning financial goals with a commitment to social and environmental well-being, readers can contribute to positive change through their everyday financial decisions.

## The Role of Philanthropy in Wealth Distribution

Philanthropy is a powerful means of redistributing wealth and creating positive change. This part of the chapter explores the role of philanthropy in wealth distribution, highlighting the impact of charitable giving on both individuals and communities. By strategically incorporating philanthropy into financial plans, individuals can leverage their resources to address pressing social and environmental challenges.

## Building Sustainable Business Practices

For entrepreneurs and business leaders, building sustainable business practices is key to aligning financial success with positive impact. This section examines how businesses can integrate ethical, social, and environmental considerations into their operations. By fostering sustainable practices, businesses can contribute to a more equitable and environmentally conscious global economy.

## Balancing Financial Goals with Environmental Stewardship

Environmental stewardship is an integral aspect of sustainable wealth. This part of the chapter explores how individuals can balance their financial goals with a commitment to environmental well-being. From sustainable consumption choices to eco-friendly investments, readers will discover ways to minimize their ecological footprint while pursuing financial prosperity.

## Fostering Inclusive Prosperity

Inclusive prosperity emphasizes the importance of ensuring that financial success is accessible to a broader spectrum of society. This section delves into the concept of fostering inclusive prosperity, examining how financial decisions can contribute to reducing economic disparities. By championing inclusivity in financial practices, individuals can play a role in creating a more just and equitable economic landscape.

## Measuring Impact and Creating a Legacy

Measuring the impact of financial choices is a crucial step in creating a meaningful legacy.

This chapter concludes by guiding readers on how to assess and measure the impact of their financial decisions. By cultivating an awareness of the lasting imprint they leave on the world, individuals can craft a legacy that reflects their values and commitment to sustainable wealth.

In the final chapters, we will explore advanced financial strategies, legacy planning, and the ongoing journey of mindful money. The path to holistic financial well being continues, with each chapter offering actionable insights for building a resilient, prosperous, and impactful financial future.

# 9 THE ONGOING JOURNEY OF MINDFUL MONEY

**Reflecting on the Journey**

As we approach the culmination of this book, it's essential to reflect on the transformative journey of mindful money. This chapter invites readers to revisit key insights, acknowledge personal growth, and celebrate the progress made on their financial path. Reflection serves as a powerful tool for learning and continued self-improvement.

**Advanced Financial Strategies for Long-Term Success**

This section explores advanced financial strategies that can elevate one's financial journey. From tax-efficient investing to estate planning, readers will gain insights into optimizing their financial decisions for long-term success. Understanding these advanced strategies empowers individuals to navigate the complexities of financial management with confidence.

## Legacy Planning: Crafting a Lasting Impact

Legacy planning goes beyond financial assets; it involves shaping a lasting impact for future generations. This part of the chapter delves into the intricacies of legacy planning, from preserving family stories to philanthropic endeavors. Readers will discover how intentional planning can create a meaningful legacy that extends far beyond monetary considerations.

## The Role of Mindfulness in Wealth Preservation

Mindfulness is a valuable companion in preserving wealth. This section explores how incorporating mindfulness into financial practices can enhance wealth preservation. By staying present, making intentional decisions, and remaining adaptable to change, individuals can safeguard their financial legacy and navigate the evolving landscape of personal finance.

## Nurturing Relationships and Community

Financial well-being is intimately tied to the quality of relationships and community connections. This part of the chapter emphasizes the importance of nurturing meaningful connections and contributing to the well-being of the community. By fostering positive relationships, individuals not only enrich their lives but also create a supportive network that enhances their overall financial journey.

## Embracing Lifelong Learning and Adaptability

The financial landscape is dynamic, requiring a commitment to lifelong learning and adaptability. This section encourages readers to embrace a mindset of continuous learning, staying informed about financial trends, and adapting strategies to evolving circumstances. By remaining curious and open to new insights, individuals can navigate the ever-changing world of finance with resilience.

## Gratitude and Mindful Abundance

Gratitude is a transformative force that amplifies the sense of abundance in life. This part of the chapter explores the role of gratitude in fostering a mindset of mindful abundance. By appreciating the resources at hand and acknowledging achievements, individuals can cultivate a positive relationship with money that transcends material wealth.

## A Call to Action: Crafting Your Future

As we approach the conclusion of this book, readers are invited to take intentional steps toward crafting their financial future. This section provides practical steps for implementing mindful money practices, setting new goals, and embracing the ongoing journey of financial well-being. By translating insights into action, individuals can create a future that aligns with their values and aspirations.

## The Journey Continues

The final chapter serves as a stepping stone rather than a destination. The journey of mindful money is ongoing, evolving with each intentional decision and transformative insight. As readers embrace the principles of mindful money, they embark on a continuous voyage toward a resilient, prosperous, and purposeful financial future.

In closing, may this book inspire and guide you on your ongoing journey of mindful money. May each mindful decision and intentional choice contribute to a life rich in purpose, well-being, and abundance. The path is yours to navigate, and the journey continues with each step you take.

# ABOUT THE AUTHOR

Vana Hendy  is a seasoned wordsmith with a passion for storytelling that has captivated readers around the world. Born and raised in Nigeria, Vana Hendy  discovered the magic of words at an early age, weaving tales that transported readers to fantastical realms and stirred their imaginations.

With a degree in Marketing  from Coal City University    , Vana Hendy combines a strongacademic foundation with a natural flair for creative expression. This unique blend of knowledge and creativity is evident in herability to craft narratives that are both intellectually stimulating and emotionally resonant.

Vana Hendy has a diverse literary palette, having penned works spanning various genres, from gripping mystery novels to heartwarming romance stories. she  believes in the transformative power of storytelling, using words to inspire, entertain, and provoke thought.

www.ingramcontent.com/pod-product-compliance
Lightning Source LLC
Chambersburg PA
CBHW060211260726
48658CB00005BA/1982